The Foodies' Food & Drink Quiz

By David Kavanagh

See also: The Quick Quiz Book of Myths and Legends

Published by Dram Books
dram.books@btinternet.com

ISBN: 9781640078826

"One of the very nicest things about life is the way
we must regularly stop whatever it is we are doing
and devote our attention to eating."
- **Luciano Pavarotti**

Questions: pages 1-89
Answers: pages 91-95

1) *Appenzeller* and *Emmental* are similar cheeses both known for their distinctive what ?

    A) Blue veins
    B) Holes
    C) Overpowering smell
    D) White rind

2) *Both cheeses also originate from the same country...which one ?*

    A) Sweden
    B) Switzerland
    C) Russia
    D) Zimbabwe

3) The Italian term *'al dente'* is used to describe cooked pasta which is meant to be what ?

    A) Spicy
    B) Soft
    C) Garlicky
    D) Firm

4) If a wine is termed *'corked'*, it is what exactly ?

    A) Improved by its corking
    B) Tainted by a decaying cork
    C) Less than two years old
    D) More than two years old

5) A *bagel* is a traditional Jewish bread roll shaped like a what ?

    A) Ring
    B) Cross
    C) Square
    D) Rectangle

6) What is the name of a rather 'peppery' *red grape* used in the production of *Côtes du Rhône* wine ?

    A) Cera
    B) Supra
    C) Syrah
    D) Cyrrus

7) *In New World wine this same grape is known as what ?*

    A) Shiraz
    B) Shia
    C) Seurat
    D) Shiva

8) What is the name of the savoury Italian, pasty-like *snack* which can play host to a wide variety of fillings ?

    A) Bizone
    B) Ozone
    C) Prozone
    D) Calzone

9) *Jarlsberg* is a nutty, sweet
cheese originating from which country ?

A) Turkey
B) Norway
C) Belgium
D) Australia

10) *Pétillant* is a French term
for a wine that is slightly what ?

A) Too sweet
B) Too alcoholic
C) Sparkling
D) Boring

11) Dishes served *'au gratin'*
are usually served with grated what ?

A) Cheese
B) Horseradish
C) Carrot
D) Cabbage

12) *Zucchini* is another word
for what exactly ?

A) Courgette
B) Cauliflower
C) Edible flower
D) Brussels sprout

13) What is the sweetest form of Champagne available ?

A) Brut
B) Sec
C) Doux
D) Extra

14) *Which is the biggest bottle of Champagne you can buy ?*

A) Nebuchadnezzar
B) Jeroboam
C) Magnum
D) Methuselah

15) *How many normal sized bottles will it contain ?*

A) Sixty
B) Fourteen
C) Six
D) Twenty

16) *A Balthazar of Champagne contains how many normal-sized bottles ?*

A) Two
B) Sixteen
C) Five
D) Thirty

17) *Biltong* are traditional strips
of dried meat found where ?

    A) South America
    B) South East Asia
    C) South Africa
    D) Iceland

18) *Riesling* is a white grape used in wine
traditionally associated with which country ?

    A) Germany
    B) Kenya
    C) China
    D) Croatia

19) *Arabica* and *Robusta* are
the world's two most popular
types of what ?

    A) Tea leaf
    B) Coffee bean
    C) Banana varieties
    D) Figs

20) *Bisque* is a thick soup which is
normally made mainly from what ?

    A) Venison
    B) Veal
    C) Mutton
    D) Shellfish

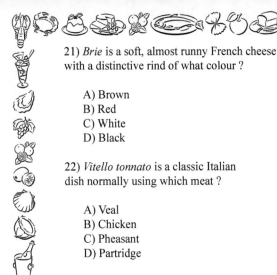

21) *Brie* is a soft, almost runny French cheese with a distinctive rind of what colour ?

A) Brown
B) Red
C) White
D) Black

22) *Vitello tonnato* is a classic Italian dish normally using which meat ?

A) Veal
B) Chicken
C) Pheasant
D) Partridge

23) *Its tasty, accompanying sauce is normally made up of caper, tuna fish and which other fish ?*

A) Cod
B) Haddock
C) Trout
D) Anchovy

24) *Conchiglie* is a variety of pasta shaped like little what ?

A) Stars
B) Shells
C) Leaves
D) Wheels

25) *Paella* is a Spanish dish that employs rice, shellfish, chicken and vegetables all coloured and flavoured by what ?

A) Beetroot
B) Melon
C) Saffron
D) Coconut

26) *Whisky* is a spirit made by distilling fermented what ?

A) Sealskin
B) Potato peelings
C) Fruit
D) Grain

27) *The Irish and American versions of this drink are spelt how ?*

A) Wisky
B) Whiskey
C) Wiskey
D) Whiscy

28) *Bourbon* is, in the main, created from what ?

A) Maize
B) Eggshells
C) Apples
D) Potatoes

29) *Zabaglione* is a delicious and popular type of what ?

A) Colombian meat dish
B) Sri Lankan fish dish
C) Indian dessert
D) Italian dessert

30) Natural grown *truffles* are highly valued, pungent and tasty what ?

A) Berries
B) Fungi
C) Flowers
D) Vines

31) *Where do truffles actually grow ?*

A) Within tree trunks
B) On branches
C) Underground
D) Underwater

32) *How many types of edible truffle are found in Europe ?*

A) Fourteen
B) Twenty one
C) Sixty
D) Three

33) What is the name of a deep-fried, triangular Indian savoury pastry pocket that holds a variety of tasty fillings ?

A) Sami
B) Alette
C) Samosa
D) Fengui

34) A *Pina Colada* is a sweet and creamy type of what ?

A) Dessert
B) Cocktail
C) Sorbet
D) Punch

35) *It is traditionally concocted with three parts what ?*

A) Custard
B) Marmalade
C) White rum
D) Red wine

36) *Tagliatelle* and *fettuccine* are types of pasta cut into what ?

A) Ribbons
B) Tubes
C) Stars
D) Ear shapes

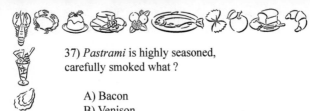

37) *Pastrami* is highly seasoned, carefully smoked what ?

    A) Bacon
    B) Venison
    C) Chicken
    D) Beef

38) *En primeur* is a phrase in French used for what ?

    A) A very old wine
    B) A very young wine
    C) A very expensive wine
    D) A very dry wine

39) *Tzatziki* is a traditional dip made from yoghurt, cucumber and garlic served where ?

    A) Argentina
    B) Bulgaria
    C) Greece
    D) Finland

40) *Gorgonzola* is a moist, blue-veined cheese best known for its what ?

    A) Bland taste
    B) Strong, pungent aroma
    C) Use in pizza
    D) Resistance to heat

41) *Which country does it traditionally hail from ?*

    A) Albania
    B) Italy
    C) Spain
    D) Romania

42) *Wine* from Australia, New Zealand, the Americas and South Africa is known as what ?

    A) Cold World
    B) Fast World
    C) New World
    D) Slow World

43) *Herbs de Provence* comprise a mixture of herbs traditionally used in which cuisine ?

    A) Indian
    B) Mediterranean
    C) Polish
    D) Irish

44) *Fusilli* pasta captures sauces by being made like little what ?

    A) Twists
    B) Butterflies
    C) Heart shapes
    D) Star shapes

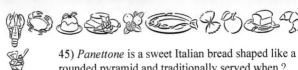

45) *Panettone* is a sweet Italian bread shaped like a rounded pyramid and traditionally served when ?

    A) The first day of Spring
    B) Easter
    C) The first day of Summer
    D) Christmas

46) What added spice or herb is used to give both flavour and heat to curries ?

    A) Tarragon
    B) Mint
    C) Basil
    D) Chilli

47) *Goulash* is a particularly rich and tasty kind of what ?

    A) Stew
    B) Ice-cream
    C) Pudding
    D) Fried fish

48) *Which country is goulash normally associated with ?*

    A) Cyprus
    B) Egypt
    C) Israel
    D) Hungary

49) *The term 'goulash' comes from a phrase meaning what ?*

    A) Dancer's teeth
    B) Herdsman's meat
    C) Singer's fish
    D) Walker's song

50) In French wine classification, *'cru'* signifies what ?

    A) Sugar content
    B) Alcohol level
    C) Growth or crop
    D) Colour

51) *Cru bourgeois means that the wines are what ?*

    A) Not classified
    B) The sweetest
    C) The lowest standard
    D) The dryest

52) *Premier cru signifies that the wines are what ?*

    A) The fruitiest taste
    B) The highest standard
    C) The lowest alcohol
    D) Bland

53) *Antipasto* is an Italian term referring to what ?

    A) Desserts
    B) Main meat dishes
    C) Main fish dishes
    D) Appetizers

54) *More literally, it infers what in particular ?*

    A) Before the meal
    B) After the meal
    C) The main course
    D) The pudding course

55) *Caviar* normally comprises the ripe eggs of which fish ?

    A) Salmon
    B) Sturgeon
    C) Bass
    D) Bream

56) *It is normally served from an iced dish on small pancakes that are called what ?*

    A) Blinis
    B) Blitz
    C) Blinks
    D) Blimps

57) *What kind of cream is the usual accompaniment?*

A) Whipped cream
B) Ice cream
C) Soured cream
D) Chocolate cream

58) *The most expensive type of caviar is called what?*

A) Minke
B) Orca
C) Blue
D) Beluga

59) *The fish that supply the most expensive caviar live mainly in which open water?*

A) Caspian and Black seas
B) Arctic Ocean
C) Red Sea
D) Pacific Ocean

60) *The most common, much cheaper substitute is what?*

A) Cod roe
B) Lumpfish roe
C) Haddock roe
D) Plaice roe

61) *Edam* is a mild, yellow and firm type of cheese which was traditionally made where ?

    A) Austria
    B) Denmark
    C) The Netherlands
    D) Mongolia

62) *It is commonly covered in a waxy rind of what colour ?*

    A) Red
    B) White
    C) Yellow
    D) Black

63) *A very similar cheese without the rind is known as what ?*

    A) Garda
    B) Gouda
    C) Gaza
    D) Gallic

64) *Non-vintage* refers to wine with no mention of what on its label ?

    A) Year of production
    B) Alcohol content
    C) Country of origin
    D) Type of wine

65) *What is the most common reason for this ?*

A) It's a blend of vintages
B) It is non-alcoholic
C) Its country is unknown
D) Its type is unclear

66) *Vichyssoise* is a traditional type of French what ?

A) Roast lamb
B) Soup
C) Stew
D) Pasta dish

67) *It is normally made with leeks, potatoes, chicken stock and what else ?*

A) Spaghetti
B) Beetroot
C) Chilli sauce
D) Cream

68) *How would it traditionally be served up to diners ?*

A) At room temperature
B) Piping hot
C) Warmed through
D) Chilled

69) *Tiramisu* is a very popular, layered type of what ?

    A) Dessert
    B) Cocktail
    C) Potato dish
    D) Fish pie

70) *Which country is it normally associated with ?*

    A) Malta
    B) Italy
    C) Nigeria
    D) Jordan

71) *Aquavit*, served chilled, is a distinctive type of what ?

    A) Non-alcoholic spirit
    B) Beer
    C) Alcoholic spirit
    D) Wine

72) *Which part of the world is it normally associated with ?*

    A) The West Indies
    B) Brazil
    C) Scandinavia
    D) Somalia

73) *It is traditionally made from what ?*

A) Grain
B) Bananas
C) Grapes
D) Coconuts

74) *Linguine* is a form of pasta shaped like what ?

A) Long, thin, flat strands
B) Little wheels
C) Long, thin, rounded strands
D) Large tubes

75) *What does the name actually mean ?*

A) Little hands
B) Long noses
C) Fiery tails
D) Small tongues

76) A flat, slightly leavened type of bread originating from the Middle East is known as what ?

A) Pipette
B) Pipi
C) Pitta
D) Pipit

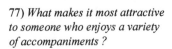

77) *What makes it most attractive
to someone who enjoys a variety
of accompaniments ?*

    A) It goes well with soup
    B) It can be split and filled
    C) It can be torn into strips
    D) It goes well with stew

78) *Hock* is an English term for
white wines from which region ?

    A) French Riviera
    B) German Rhine
    C) Swiss Alps
    D) Russian Steppes

79) *Satay* is a dish of grilled and
spiced meat served how ?

    A) Skewered on sticks
    B) Wrapped in vine leaves
    C) On a bed of noodles
    D) Under a layer of pasta

80) *Where does this dish actually
originate from ?*

    A) Eastern Europe
    B) Malaysia and Indonesia
    C) Outer Hebrides
    D) The Channel Islands

81) *What kind of sauce is the traditional accompaniment to it ?*

A) Peanut sauce
B) Apple sauce
C) Tomato sauce
D) Lemon sauce

82) *Foie gras is made from goose or duck what ?*

A) Liver
B) Heart
C) Brains
D) Gizzard

83) *How is it normally served up to diners ?*

A) Deep fried
B) Chargrilled
C) Poached or braised
D) Raw

84) *Why is it such a controversial dish for many ?*

A) The farmers are poor
B) The birds are force fed
C) Farmland is destroyed
D) The birds are pets

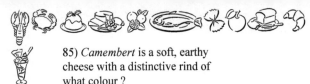

85) *Camembert* is a soft, earthy cheese with a distinctive rind of what colour ?

    A) Red
    B) White
    C) Yellow
    D) Blue

86) *Which country does this cheese hail from ?*

    A) Bolivia
    B) France
    C) Luxembourg
    D) Slovenia

87) The clear gap in a wine bottle between wine and cork is called what ?

    A) Ullage
    B) Umbrage
    C) Umber
    D) Ulna

88) *Eiswein* is a distinctive, sweet kind of what ?

    A) Grape juice
    B) Spirit
    C) Grape cocktail
    D) Wine

89) *Which country is eiswein the most associated with ?*

    A) Germany
    B) Serbia
    C) Portugal
    D) Sudan

90) *It is made from grapes that have been what ?*

    A) Crushed by wild boar
    B) Trampled by goats
    C) Picked in a heatwave
    D) Frozen by frost

91) A thick soup or stew made with shellfish and/or fish is known as a what ?

    A) Chimera
    B) Chowder
    C) Chine
    D) Chock

92) *Stilton* is a strong, distinctive cheese that can be produced in two varieties...white and what ?

    A) Orange
    B) Blue
    C) Yellow
    D) Red

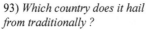

93) *Which country does it hail from traditionally ?*

    A) England
    B) Canada
    C) Wales
    D) Fiji

94) *What type of milk is normally used to make stilton ?*

    A) Cow's milk
    B) Goat's milk
    C) Rabbit's milk
    D) Sheep's milk

95) *Chorizo* is a traditional type of Spanish what ?

    A) Bread
    B) Burger
    C) Sausage
    D) Fish tart

96) *What does chorizo mainly consist of ?*

    A) Wheat flour and butter
    B) Minced veal
    C) Raw tuna
    D) Cured pork or beef

97) *It is often added to a Spanish white bean stew called what ?*

    A) Falia
    B) Fandango
    C) Fanta
    D) Fabada

98) *Sauvignon Blanc* is a grape type used mostly to make what ?

    A) Sweet red wine
    B) Dry white wine
    C) Dry red wine
    D) Perry

99) *Tofu*, or *bean curd*, is the white purée derivation of what exactly ?

    A) Flageolet beans
    B) Soya beans
    C) Borlotti beans
    D) Haricot beans

100) *It is high in protein and also particularly popular among which group of people ?*

    A) Hunters
    B) Vegetarians
    C) Fishermen
    D) Singers

101) *In which country has tofu now become a staple food ?*

    A) Japan
    B) New Zealand
    C) Jamaica
    D) Panama

102) Which aromatic herb is the most commonly used with onion to make a stuffing ?

    A) Rosemary
    B) Marjoram
    C) Dill
    D) Sage

103) *Cognac* is a type of brandy made from the double distilling of what ?

    A) Vodka
    B) White wine
    C) Cider
    D) Red wine

104) *How is cognac matured for up to 60 years ?*

    A) In glass barrels
    B) In underground silos
    C) In sheepskin flasks
    D) In seasoned oak casks

105) *Where is Cognac, the town, that gives the drink its name ?*

    A) California, USA
    B) Czech Republic
    C) Western France
    D) Estonia

106) What is the name of the *cocktail* which comprises two parts gin or vodka with orange juice ?

    A) A Screwdriver
    B) A Piledriver
    C) A Latin Lover
    D) A Train Driver

107) *Sashimi* is a dish of thinly sliced, raw what ?

    A) Beef
    B) Fish
    C) Venison
    D) Turkey

108) *Which country is sashimi most associated with ?*

    A) Algeria
    B) Barbados
    C) Cameroon
    D) Japan

109) *What type of sauce is the traditional accompaniment ?*

    A) Soy sauce
    B) Orange sauce
    C) Tomato sauce
    D) Garlic sauce

110) *Polenta* is a particular type of Italian what ?

    A) Cornmeal
    B) Pasta dish
    C) Sausage
    D) Steak

111) *How is polenta normally prepared for being eaten ?*

    A) Boiled or baked
    B) Deep fried
    C) Pan fried
    D) Just washed

112) *Spumante*, as in *Martini Spumante* or *Asti Spumante*, is Italian for what ?

    A) Flat
    B) Sugary
    C) Cold
    D) Sparkling

113) What is the name of the *fungus* used to produce the honeyed sweetness of various sweet white wines such as *Sauternes* ?

A) Noble rot
B) Honest grot
C) Cheeky rot
D) Bold grot

114) *Lasagne* is a particular type of pasta served how ?

A) In parcels
B) In sheets
C) In long, flat strands
D) In leaf shapes

115) *Pretzels* are a typically dry, crusty form of what ?

A) Meat
B) Fish
C) Bread
D) Fruit

116) *Which country do pretzels originate from ?*

A) Ecuador
B) Ethiopia
C) Germany
D) Monaco

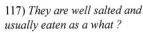

117) *They are well salted and usually eaten as a what ?*

    A) Main meal
    B) Dessert
    C) Snack
    D) Starter

118) *Prosciutto* is a traditional type of Italian what ?

    A) Cured ham
    B) Fizzy white wine
    C) Cured beef
    D) Fizzy red wine

119) *How long is prosciutto generally matured for ?*

    A) Two to three days
    B) Eight months to two years
    C) One to two months
    D) Six to seven months

120) *What is the most famous version of prosciutto ?*

    A) Karma
    B) Lorna
    C) Parma
    D) Starma

121) A *leavened* type of Indian flatbread typically served with curry is known as what ?

A) Flan
B) Nan
C) Fran
D) Man

122) *This flatbread is traditionally shaped like a what ?*

A) Teardrop
B) Banana
C) Square
D) Triangle

123) *How is it usually cooked in keeping with tradition ?*

A) Over an open fire
B) In a shallow pan
C) In a deep fat fryer
D) In a tandoori oven

124) *Ruote* is a type of pasta that is shaped like mini what ?

A) Leaves
B) Shells
C) Pens
D) Wheels

125) *Saffron* is an expensive spice derived from which flowers ?

    A) Roses
    B) Begonias
    C) Crocuses
    D) Daffodils

126) *From which part of a flower does saffron come ?*

    A) Seeds
    B) Leaves
    C) Stigmas
    D) Stems

127) *Gnocchi* are tasty, savoury little Italian what ?

    A) Dumplings
    B) Cupcakes
    C) Pies
    D) Chicken pieces

128) *They are traditionally served with what kind of sauce ?*

    A) Tomato sauce
    B) Chilli sauce
    C) Onion sauce
    D) Apple sauce

129) A traditional *Dry Martini* is a cocktail comprising two parts gin to one part what ?

A) Sweet sherry
B) Dry vermouth
C) Sweet cider
D) Perry

130) *What fruit or vegetable is a common accompaniment to this cocktail ?*

A) A slice of cucumber
B) A green olive
C) A slice of lime
D) A horseradish

131) A *kebab* is made from chunks of meat or vegetables cooked how ?

A) In a frying pan
B) On a hot plate
C) On a skewer
D) In a clay oven

132) *A doner kebab is normally made from slices of spit-roasted what ?*

A) Venison
B) Lamb
C) Camel
D) Pork

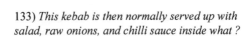

133) *This kebab is then normally served up with salad, raw onions, and chilli sauce inside what ?*

    A) A pitta bread
    B) Vine leaves
    C) A toasted bun
    D) Wholemeal toast

134) What is the name of a *white grape* used for *Champagne*, *Burgundy* and several *New World white wines* ?

    A) Charabanc
    B) Chariot
    C) Chervil
    D) Chardonnay

135) *Ravioli* is a type of pasta made to look like little what ?

    A) Stars
    B) Faces
    C) Crosses
    D) Parcels

136) What is the name of the *nutty flavoured spice* often used in milk puddings and the like ?

    A) Nutshell
    B) Nutria
    C) Nutmeg
    D) Nuzzle

137) *Grappa* is a strong, clear spirit originating from which country ?

    A) Italy
    B) Mexico
    C) Nicaragua
    D) Trinidad and Tobago

138) *What is grappa made from by traditional producers ?*

    A) Distilled wine grape remains
    B) Fermented melons
    C) Distilled potatoes
    D) Fermented banana skins

139) What is the name of a soft, white Italian cheese often made from *water buffalo's milk* ?

    A) Mau Mau
    B) Mozzarella
    C) Maximo
    D) Mazzini

140) *This cheese is commonly used to make the tasty, stringy toppings for what ?*

    A) Cakes
    B) Pizzas
    C) Pies
    D) Fish dishes

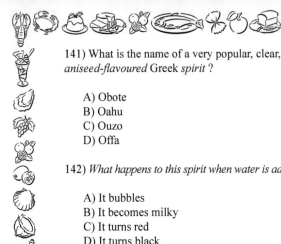

141) What is the name of a very popular, clear, *aniseed-flavoured* Greek *spirit* ?

    A) Obote
    B) Oahu
    C) Ouzo
    D) Offa

142) *What happens to this spirit when water is added ?*

    A) It bubbles
    B) It becomes milky
    C) It turns red
    D) It turns black

143) What is the name given to fine, *matchstick vegetable strips* used as a garnish, salad or even cooked in butter ?

    A) Julienne
    B) Julius Caesar
    C) Juneau
    D) Jung

144) A famed *cocktail* made with vodka, orange juice, Galliano liqueur and crushed ice is known as a what ?

    A) Titus Ballbreaker
    B) Hairy Bulldozer
    C) Metal Headbanger
    D) Harvey Wallbanger

145) *Farfalle* is a type of pasta which most looks like which creatures ?

A) Lions
B) Butterflies
C) Sharks
D) Snakes

146) *What is often added to this pasta to change its colour before cooking ?*

A) Lemon or orange
B) Peach or melon
C) Tomato or spinach
D) Carrot or turnip

147) What is the name for a Spanish selection of savoury, tasty *hors d'oeuvre* ?

A) Tahini
B) Tapas
C) Taboo
D) Tantala

148) What is the French word for *'little nut'* often used to describe small, boned lamb steaks ?

A) Nihili
B) Nirvana
C) Nurmi
D) Noisette

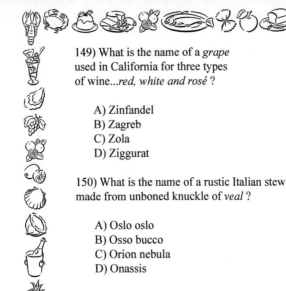

149) What is the name of a *grape* used in California for three types of wine...*red, white and rosé* ?

    A) Zinfandel
    B) Zagreb
    C) Zola
    D) Ziggurat

150) What is the name of a rustic Italian stew made from unboned knuckle of *veal* ?

    A) Oslo oslo
    B) Osso bucco
    C) Orion nebula
    D) Onassis

151) *Cannelloni* is a type of pasta shaped like what ?

    A) Tiny tubes
    B) Wheels
    C) Large tubes
    D) Petals

152) *What accompaniment is the most traditional with this pasta ?*

    A) Lamb chops and gravy
    B) Venison steaks
    C) Fish balls
    D) Meat filling and sauce

153) What is the name of a dry, golden-brown *brandy* distilled in Gers, France ?

A) Armada
B) Armagnac
C) Armadillo
D) Arrack

154) *Up to how long will this drink be left to mature ?*

A) Six months
B) Forty years
C) Eighteen years
D) Five years

155) *Bombay 'duck'*, found off the west coast of India, is actually a type of what ?

A) Turtle
B) Dolphin
C) Small fish
D) Octopus

156) *How is this 'duck' prepared before it is flavoured and eaten ?*

A) It is dried in the sun
B) It is buried underground
C) It is allowed to rot
D) It is soaked in gin

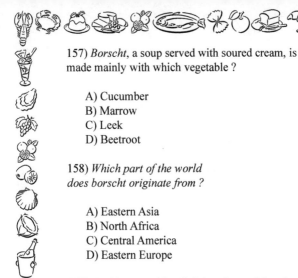

157) *Borscht*, a soup served with soured cream, is made mainly with which vegetable ?

    A) Cucumber
    B) Marrow
    C) Leek
    D) Beetroot

158) *Which part of the world does borscht originate from ?*

    A) Eastern Asia
    B) North Africa
    C) Central America
    D) Eastern Europe

159) A white, crumbly, slightly salty traditional Greek cheese is called what ?

    A) Fettle
    B) Feta
    C) Feu
    D) Fez

160) What is the name of the triangular Turkish/ Greek sweet combining layers of thin pastry with chopped almonds, pistachios, sugar and spices ?

    A) Bacchus
    B) Bach
    C) Baklava
    D) Balkan

161) *Dauphinoise* is a French way
of oven-baking what ?

    A) Potatoes
    B) Lamb hearts
    C) Pork chops
    D) Stuffed tomatoes

162) *How are they traditionally
prepared for the table ?*

    A) Thinly sliced with cream
    B) Minced with onion
    C) On a bed of rice
    D) Mashed with herbs

163) A *cocktail* made with one part lime juice,
four parts white rum, plus sugar and crushed ice
is called a what ?

    A) Descartes
    B) Daiquiri
    C) Defoe
    D) Darius

164) *Focaccia* is a soft, savoury
type of Italian what ?

    A) Fish pasta
    B) Potato dish
    C) Flat bread
    D) Pasty

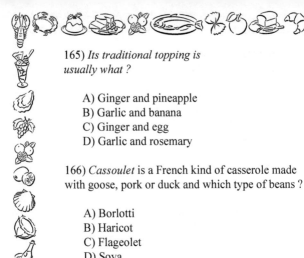

165) *Its traditional topping is usually what ?*

    A) Ginger and pineapple
    B) Garlic and banana
    C) Ginger and egg
    D) Garlic and rosemary

166) *Cassoulet* is a French kind of casserole made with goose, pork or duck and which type of beans ?

    A) Borlotti
    B) Haricot
    C) Flageolet
    D) Soya

167) What is the name of a very popular hard, salty Italian type of cheese ?

    A) Parietal
    B) Pomerol
    C) Potsdam
    D) Parmesan

168) *How is this cheese most commonly used for a dish ?*

    A) Melted for dipping
    B) Deep fried in batter
    C) Cut into chunks
    D) Freshly grated

169) A meat *preserve* made by slowly cooking a piece of meat in its own fat – often duck – is known as a what ?

A) Confit
B) Contort
C) Contra
D) Conino

170) *What is then used to seal and store the meat traditionally in an air-tight pot ?*

A) Layers of bacon
B) Melted cheese
C) More of the same fat
D) Layers of fruit

171) *Ghee*, clarified butter made from cow or buffalo's milk, is extensively used where ?

A) Angola
B) Belize
C) India
D) Chile

172) A *croissant* is a popular and tasty French what ?

A) Cupcake
B) Biscuit
C) Pastry
D) Ice cream

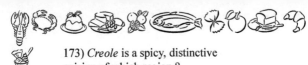

173) *Creole* is a spicy, distinctive cuisine of which region ?

    A) The West Indies
    B) Western Russia
    C) Central Africa
    D) Southern Asia

174) *Gravad lax*, a Scandinavian dish, comprises thinly sliced and marinated what ?

    A) Mushrooms
    B) Raw salmon
    C) Hard-boiled eggs
    D) Raw beef

175) *What kind of sauce is its traditional accompaniment ?*

    A) Mustard and dill
    B) Tomato
    C) Chilli
    D) Garlic and orange

176) *Bratwurst* is a popular and traditional German what ?

    A) Bread
    B) Pie
    C) Sausage
    D) Pudding

44

177) *What, finely chopped, goes into it normally ?*

    A) Almonds and peanuts
    B) Peaches and pears
    C) Beef, pork or veal
    D) Cod or herring

178) What is the name of a very strong Mexican *spirit* made from the pulp of a plant ?

    A) Tequila
    B) Technetium
    C) Tempera
    D) Teme

179) *Besides a slice of lemon or lime, what else is the traditional accompaniment to this spirit when served ?*

    A) A pinch of ginger
    B) A pinch of garlic
    C) A pinch of salt
    D) A pinch of chilli

180) The four principal *northern* wine-making regions of France are Alsace, Loire, Chablis and what else ?

    A) Burgundy
    B) Champagne
    C) Bordeaux
    D) Côtes du Rhône

181) *Quill-shaped* pasta, often served with a spicy sauce, is known as what ?

    A) Jenne
    B) Lenne
    C) Benne
    D) Penne

182) A Japanese savoury dish comprising *seaweed* filled with rice and raw fish is called what ?

    A) Sushi
    B) Surd
    C) Suzerain
    D) Swanndri

183) *What is the traditional accompaniment to this dish ?*

    A) Pickled ginger/horseradish
    B) Fried garlic and thyme
    C) Slices of apple/plums
    D) Beef and onion gravy

184) *Meze*, or *mezze*, in Turkey or Greece, is a traditional selection of what ?

    A) Cocktails
    B) Spiced hors d'oeuvre
    C) Puddings
    D) Rare steaks

185) *The word itself is actually Turkish for what ?*

    A) Gentlemen's relish
    B) Small bite
    C) Juicy drinks
    D) Delicious meat

186) *Okra*, a green vegetable with a light flavour and soft, seeded centre is colloquially called what ?

    A) Girls' stomachs
    B) Ladies' fingers
    C) Boys' stomachs
    D) Ladies' hair

187) *Cassis*, a sweet liqueur, is traditionally made from which fruit ?

    A) Apricots
    B) Limes
    C) Blackcurrants
    D) Lemons

188) *Mixed with Champagne, it is known as what ?*

    A) Kir Royale
    B) Kir Mono
    C) Kir Spumante
    D) Kir Blanc

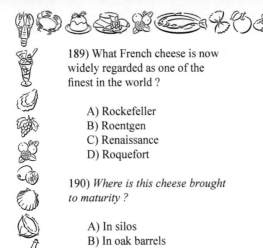

189) What French cheese is now widely regarded as one of the finest in the world ?

A) Rockefeller
B) Roentgen
C) Renaissance
D) Roquefort

190) *Where is this cheese brought to maturity ?*

A) In silos
B) In oak barrels
C) In fridges
D) In caves

191) *Macaroni* pasta is normally shaped like what ?

A) Small curved tubes
B) Buttons
C) Large curved tubes
D) Pillows

192) *Sauerkraut*, a German dish, mainly comprises shredded what ?

A) Beef
B) Pork
C) Cabbage
D) Beetroot

193) A Japanese way to grill marinated fish or meat over charcoal is termed what ?

A) Tanganyika
B) Talmud
C) Teriyaki
D) Tatars

194) A pink wine, usually made from the juice of red grapes, is commonly known as what ?

A) Robart
B) Rosé
C) Razin
D) Rosetta

195) *Americans often refer to this same wine as what ?*

A) Bellini
B) Blurt
C) Belle
D) Blush

196) *Pesto* is an Italian sauce that is traditionally made from cheese, garlic, basil, olive oil and what else ?

A) Pine nuts
B) Orange peel
C) Lemon rind
D) Peanuts

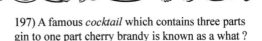

197) A famous *cocktail* which contains three parts gin to one part cherry brandy is known as a what ?

    A) Cambodia Ripper
    B) Peruvian Banger
    C) Singapore Sling
    D) London Harp

198) *Felafel* is a traditional Middle Eastern dish of what ?

    A) Deep fried patties
    B) Goat meat
    C) Camel meat
    D) Roasted vegetables

199) *What does this dish actually consist of ?*

    A) Minced goat haunch
    B) Spiced beans or chickpeas
    C) Carrots and leeks
    D) Camel hump steaks

200) *How is this dish normally offered to diners ?*

    A) On skewers
    B) In a soup
    C) In an omelette
    D) In pitta bread

201) What is reputed to be the most widely used *herb* in the world ?

    A) Coriander
    B) Thyme
    C) Parsley
    D) Basil

202) The French term *'en croûte'* means a dish cooked how ?

    A) Over a naked flame
    B) In a clay oven
    C) In a pastry case
    D) Over charcoal

203) A *purée* of vegetables/fruit, thin enough to pour, is known as a what ?

    A) Coop
    B) Coulis
    C) Cornice
    D) Copra

204) A famous *cocktail* made with four parts tequila to two parts lemon or lime juice is called a what ?

    A) Majenta
    B) Maidenhead
    C) Margarita
    D) Majesty

205) *What traditional addition is made to the glass this cocktail is served in ?*

A) Chilli around the rim
B) Salt around the rim
C) Garlic around the rim
D) Pepper around the rim

206) A *white stew* made of lamb, chicken or veal in a cream sauce is known as a what ?

A) Blarney
B) Blanquette
C) Blether
D) Blancmange

207) A *consommé* is a clear, thin soup made from what ?

A) Fruit juice
B) Coconut milk
C) Egg whites
D) Clarified stock

208) What is the name of a type of *unleavened* Indian bread that is made from coarse, wholemeal flour ?

A) Chomsky
B) Cimabue
C) Ceres
D) Chapatti

209) Worldwide, *spaghetti* is now generally reputed to be what ?

A) The most popular pasta
B) The tastiest pasta
C) The least popular pasta
D) The hardest pasta to cook

210) Both *powdered* and *fresh root* versions of what are now commonly used in curries and stir fries ?

A) Oregano
B) Cloves
C) Ginger
D) Chervil

211) *En papillote* is a method of cooking and serving food how ?

A) In thick pastry
B) In oiled or buttered paper/foil
C) Wrapped in leaves
D) Covered in salt

212) *What is thought to be the main attraction of this method ?*

A) It is more hygienic
B) It keeps in juices and flavours
C) It wards off evil spirits
D) It is much faster

213) Who was the British *writer* who wrote a definitive *Victorian* guide to cookery/housekeeping ?

A) Mr Beeton
B) Mrs Seaton
C) Mrs Beeton
D) Mr Seaton

214) *This writer died relatively young...*
what were the years of birth and death ?

A) 1836-1865
B) 1802-1842
C) 1901-1933
D) 1907-1945

215) *Hors d'oeuvre* comprising raw vegetables cut into sticks and eaten with dips, are called what ?

A) Croutons
B) Crudités
C) Cruxes
D) Croziers

216) What is the name of a hard, gold-coloured, popular type of *English* cheese ?

A) Cedar
B) Cellar
C) Cheddar
D) Chipper

217) *What natural ingredient is its basis ?*

A) Sheep's milk
B) Goat's milk
C) Cow's milk
D) Buffalo's milk

218) *For at least how long is this cheese normally matured for ?*

A) Five to six days
B) Two to three months
C) Four to six weeks
D) Twelve to 18 months

219) What is the name of a very adaptable *grape variety* used in wines from France, Italy, eastern Europe and the New World ?

A) Merlin
B) Merlot
C) Merino
D) Meridien

220) *Which type of blended wine is this grape mostly used for in France ?*

A) Red Bordeaux
B) Beaujolais
C) Sauternes
D) Red Burgundies

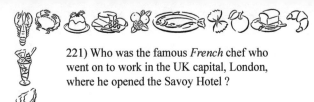

221) Who was the famous *French* chef who went on to work in the UK capital, London, where he opened the Savoy Hotel ?

    A) Fabergé
    B) Defoe
    C) Escoffier
    D) Degas

222) *What were the dates of this character's birth and death ?*

    A) 1747-1836
    B) 1901-1955
    C) 1847-1935
    D) 1801-1860

223) *What was the name of the famous dessert he invented ?*

    A) Peach Melba
    B) Orange Twist
    C) Raspberry Ripple
    D) Lemon Tart

224) *In whose honour was this delicious dish named ?*

    A) A female Australian soprano
    B) A male American tenor
    C) A female Pakistani alto
    D) A male Austrian baritone

225) In the UK, *red Bordeaux* wine is traditionally referred to as what ?

A) Claret
B) Clarence
C) Clod
D) Claque

226) *Gazpacho* is a popular and traditional Spanish what ?

A) Bread
B) Lobster salad dish
C) Roast lamb dish
D) Soup

227) *How is it normally served up to diners ?*

A) Fresh out of the oven
B) At room temperature
C) Re-heated after going cold
D) Chilled or iced

228) A popular *curry spice* with a medium hot, strong taste is known as what ?

A) Comma
B) Cumin
C) Cubit
D) Cumquat

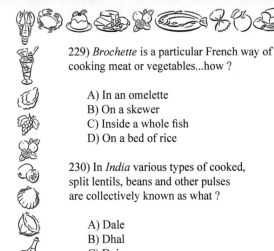

229) *Brochette* is a particular French way of cooking meat or vegetables...how ?

    A) In an omelette
    B) On a skewer
    C) Inside a whole fish
    D) On a bed of rice

230) In *India* various types of cooked, split lentils, beans and other pulses are collectively known as what ?

    A) Dale
    B) Dhal
    C) Dais
    D) Dinar

231) An *enchilada* is a tasty, spicy Mexican what ?

    A) Corn pancake
    B) Chicken leg
    C) Cocktail
    D) Ice cream

232) *How is it normally served up to diners ?*

    A) In a tall glass with a cherry
    B) With a slice of cake
    C) Filled with meat or beans
    D) With braised chicken liver

233) *What is its traditional topping before being consumed ?*

    A) Two types of jam
    B) Chicken gravy
    C) Chilli sauce and cheese
    D) Apple sauce

234) A salty *purée* of anchovies, black olives, capers, garlic and lemon juice is known as a what ?

    A) Tamarind
    B) Tansy
    C) Tapioca
    D) Tapenade

235) *How is this purée the most commonly used ?*

    A) In milk puddings
    B) In pasta sauces
    C) On sandwiches
    D) On fruit salads

236) *Pilaf*, or *pilau*, is a special Eastern method of cooking what ?

    A) Rice
    B) Potatoes
    C) Mutton leg
    D) Goat steaks

237) *Fromage frais* is a certain type of cheese especially known for its what ?

    A) Blue veins
    B) Lightness of taste
    C) Red rind
    D) Strong odour

238) *This cheese is often used as a substitute for what ?*

    A) Vegetable purée
    B) Cream
    C) Fruit purée
    D) Jelly

239) *Bouillabaisse* is a traditional soup or stew made mainly with what ?

    A) Pork fillets and pork stock
    B) Chicken and mushrooms
    C) Fish fillets and fish stock
    D) Lamb and oranges

240) *Black bouillabaisse is a particular variation of this dish containing what ?*

    A) Venison cutlets
    B) Pheasant giblets
    C) Cuttlefish and its ink
    D) Sheep's intestines

241) *Chèvre* is a white, crumbly, creamy French cheese made from which main ingredient ?

A) Rabbit's milk
B) Sheep's milk
C) Buffalo's milk
D) Goat's milk

242) *How is this cheese usually produced for eating ?*

A) In large cubes
B) In ring shapes
C) In triangles
D) In small rolls

243) The term *'Appellation Contrôlée'* on any French wine relates to what ?

A) Its source
B) Its strength
C) Its sweetness
D) Its colour

244) A big *Scandinavian* selection of savoury dishes, served hot or cold, is known as a what ?

A) Stromboli
B) Smorgasbord
C) Stroessner
D) Sonoma

245) *Shiitake*, often used in Oriental stir fries and elsewhere, are a type of what ?

 A) Onion
 B) Nut
 C) Mushroom
 D) Ginger plant

246) The vegetables of the *gourd* family are collectively known as what ?

 A) Squish
 B) Squelch
 C) Squiggle
 D) Squash

247) *Which of these does not belong in the gourd family ?*

 A) Courgette
 B) Pumpkin
 C) Potato
 D) Marrow

248) Which country does the *Gewürztraminer* wine-producing grape hail from ?

 A) South Africa
 B) Lebanon
 C) Germany
 D) Latvia

249) *Dolmades* consists of minced lamb and rice traditionally rolled into what ?

    A) Lettuce leaves
    B) Vine leaves
    C) Cabbage leaves
    D) Banana leaves

250) *Which part of the world does this dish originate from ?*

    A) Greece and Turkey
    B) Thailand
    C) Tonga
    D) Zambia

251) *Couscous*, a popular food, is made from coarsely ground, hard what ?

    A) Oats
    B) Barley
    C) Pumpkin
    D) Wheat

252) *In which part of the world is it a staple part of the daily diet ?*

    A) Papua New Guinea
    B) Southern Russia
    C) Scandinavia
    D) North Africa

253) The *carob bean* is often used as a substitute for what in dishes ?

    A) Garlic
    B) Chocolate
    C) Ginger
    D) Salt

254) *Why is its substitution thought to be healthier ?*

    A) Lower fat content/no caffeine
    B) Less salty
    C) Not as pungent/smelly
    D) Better for digestion

255) *Cordon bleu* is a term often used in cooking meaning what ?

    A) A very high standard
    B) An average standard
    C) A very low standard
    D) Not classified

256) *What does the term mean in a literal sense ?*

    A) Blue ribbon
    B) Red ribbon
    C) Blue sword
    D) Yellow arrow

257) *Historically, in France, it was used to refer to what ?*

    A) The peasantry
    B) The top order of knighthood
    C) The castle cook
    D) The best archer

258) A popular, rich *sauce* which comprises egg yolk, butter and lemon juice – often served with fish or egg dishes – is called what ?

    A) Honeydew
    B) Holmium
    C) Hollyhock
    D) Hollandaise

259) *Entremets* is a French dining term referring to dishes that are served how ?

    A) Inside other dishes
    B) Brought to the table alight
    C) Between main courses
    D) To a loud fanfare

260) *What kind of offerings might this refer to ?*

    A) A duck inside a goose
    B) Brandy pudding
    C) A sorbet or small salad
    D) A celebratory, display dish

261) What is the name of an aromatic plant whose liquorice-flavoured *seeds* are used to flavour food and drink ?

A) Anise
B) Amok
C) Amphora
D) Amethyst

262) *Which drinks are these seeds typically used to flavour ?*

A) Ginger ale and ginger wine
B) Red Bordeaux
C) Red Burgundies
D) Pastis and ouzo

263) Which country does the spicy and herby *'bhaji'* vegetable dish hail from ?

A) Armenia
B) Bahamas
C) India
D) Belarus

264) *Onion bhajis are rolled into balls and covered in what before being deep fried ?*

A) Peanut sauce
B) Crushed pine nuts
C) Flour
D) Boiled rice

265) *Muscat* is a white grape variety traditionally used by wine producers where ?

A) Spain
B) Hungary
C) France
D) Senegal

266) *In which other country is Muscat traditionally employed to make Asti Spumante ?*

A) Italy
B) Portugal
C) Greece
D) Libya

267) *Boudin blanc* is a delicately spiced French what ?

A) Sausage
B) Bread roll
C) Rice dish
D) Meat pie

268) *Boudin noir is the French equivalent of British what ?*

A) Black pudding
B) Yorkshire pudding
C) Bread pudding
D) Rice pudding

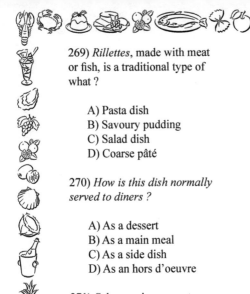

269) *Rillettes*, made with meat or fish, is a traditional type of what ?

    A) Pasta dish
    B) Savoury pudding
    C) Salad dish
    D) Coarse pâté

270) *How is this dish normally served to diners ?*

    A) As a dessert
    B) As a main meal
    C) As a side dish
    D) As an hors d'oeuvre

271) *Schnapps* is a very strong German type of what ?

    A) Beer
    B) Spirit
    C) Red wine
    D) White wine

272) *What is normally used in the production process to make it ?*

    A) A variety of fruit
    B) A selection of nuts
    C) Vegetable peelings
    D) Hops

273) *How is it traditionally served to drinkers ?*

    A) Ice cold
    B) Piping hot
    C) At room temperature
    D) Warmed through

274) *Bourguignon* is a method of cooking food in what ?

    A) Its own fat
    B) Red wine
    C) Whisky
    D) Fruit juice

275) *Ciabatta* is a popular and distinctive type of what ?

    A) Spaghetti dish
    B) Meat loaf
    C) White bread
    D) Summer salad

276) *Which country is ciabatta traditionally associated with ?*

    A) Gambia
    B) Morocco
    C) Uruguay
    D) Italy

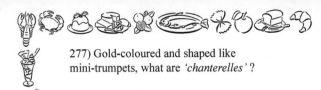

277) Gold-coloured and shaped like mini-trumpets, what are *'chanterelles'* ?

    A) Edible flowers
    B) Tiny cabbages
    C) Mushrooms
    D) A type of nut

278) What is the name of a dish made, served or garnished with *spinach* and coated in a *Mornay* sauce ?

    A) Roman
    B) Florentine
    C) Venetian
    D) Milanese

279) *What are the historic origins behind the city's links ?*

    A) Spinach was banned there
    B) Spinach was a regional crop
    C) Spinach was unknown there
    D) Spinach was just animal feed

280) *Taramasalata* is a rich purée dish made from what ?

    A) Smoked cod's roe
    B) Pickled eggs
    C) Smoked eel
    D) Pickled lamb's testicles

281) *Which country does it hail from originally ?*

    A) Greece
    B) Tunisia
    C) Ukraine
    D) Uganda

282) *Blended with olive oil and lemon juice, what is its normal colour ?*

    A) Dark red
    B) Pale pink
    C) Dark green
    D) Black

283) What grape variety is used to make *red Burgundy* wines ?

    A) Pinot Noir
    B) Pinot Nouvelle
    C) Pinot Nigra
    D) Pinot Nabis

284) What is the thick sesame seed *paste* used in Greek and Lebanese cooking ?

    A) Tahiti
    B) Taipan
    C) Tamil
    D) Tahini

285) *In which common dish is it an important ingredient ?*

A) Hummock
B) Humbug
C) Hummous
D) Humerus

286) *What usually accompanies it to create this common dish ?*

A) Devilled kidneys
B) Diced carrots
C) Puréed chickpeas
D) Sliced apples

287) A traditional, thick *soup* made in Louisiana, southern USA, is known as what ?

A) Grilse
B) Gunny
C) Gumbo
D) Guzzle

288) *What vegetable is the usual mainstay of this soup ?*

A) Cucumber
B) Marrow
C) Okra
D) Lettuce

72

289) *Kedgeree* is a traditional breakfast dish comprising rice, hard-boiled egg, onions and what else ?

A) Bacon
B) Beef
C) Lamb
D) Fish

290) *What form does this final component traditionally come in ?*

A) Smoky bacon
B) Rare lamb steak
C) Raw beef steak
D) Smoked haddock

291) *Haggis* is an old traditional dish comprising oatmeal, onions, fat and spicy offal all wrapped in a what ?

A) Banana leaf
B) Sheep's stomach
C) Cabbage leaf
D) Horse's stomach

292) *Which country has haggis long been associated with ?*

A) Wales
B) Scotland
C) Ireland
D) England

293) *Which time of the year is it traditionally served ?*

    A) Christmas Eve, December 24
    B) Burns Night, January 25
    C) St Patrick's Day, March 17
    D) St George's Day, April 23

294) *Guacamole* is a Mexican dish comprising crushed tomato, seasoning and mashed what ?

    A) Avocado
    B) Pear
    C) Leek
    D) Artichoke

295) *It is normally served with thin cornmeal pancakes known as what ?*

    A) Torques
    B) Tortillas
    C) Tonsures
    D) Toreadors

296) A *'macrobiotic'* diet aimed at healthy living forbids which three key dietary groups ?

    A) Grains, fruit and alcohol
    B) Fish, grains and vegetables
    C) Meat, fruit and alcohol
    D) Meat, fish and grains

297) *The diet is historically taken from which belief system ?*

A) Roman Catholicism
B) Judaism
C) Zen Buddhism
D) Islam

298) *Fondue* is a Swiss speciality of dipping cubes of bread or meat into a dish predominantly of what ?

A) Grated cheese
B) Onion gravy
C) Lemon juice
D) Melted cheese

299) *Bresaola* is an Italian dish comprising cured, dried what ?

A) Beef tenderloin
B) Pig's liver
C) Venison haunch
D) Turkey breast

300) *How long is it traditionally dried for ?*

A) Two months
B) Two years
C) Two weeks
D) Two days

301) *How is it then normally served up to diners ?*

    A) In thick chunks
    B) Minced
    C) Sliced thinly
    D) In pastry cases

302) *Morels* and *ceps* are two distinctive types of what ?

    A) Bean
    B) Radish
    C) Pea
    D) Mushroom

303) *Niçoise* is a word describing dishes originating from which part of the world ?

    A) Nicosia, Cyprus
    B) Nicaragua
    C) Nice and south east France
    D) Nice, California, USA

304) *These dishes are typically made with tomatoes, olives, garlic, green beans and what else ?*

    A) Salmon
    B) Grated ginger
    C) Anchovies
    D) Grated cheese

305) *Bulgur* is a distinct, nutty-flavoured type of what ?

A) Cracked wheat
B) Truffle
C) Rolled oat
D) Fish roe

306) *Steamed bulgur is used as the basis of a cold Middle East dish known as what ?*

A) Tabbouleh
B) Taco
C) Tableau
D) Tabalco

307) *Raclette* is a traditional dish involving melted cheese which comes from where ?

A) Poland
B) Switzerland
C) Denmark
D) Norway

308) *Typically, raclette is eaten with potatoes, pickles and what else ?*

A) Gherkins
B) Mashed turnip
C) Fried rice
D) Banana

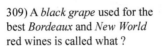

309) A *black grape* used for the
best *Bordeaux* and *New World*
red wines is called what ?

    A) Cabernet Noir
    B) Gamay
    C) Chardonnay Noir
    D) Cabernet Sauvignon

310) A *pot-au-feu* is one meal that
can be served in which two parts ?

    A) Soup and dessert
    B) Main dish and dessert
    C) Soup and main dish
    D) Dessert and coffee

311) *From which country does it
originate ?*

    A) France
    B) Bulgaria
    C) St Lucia
    D) Mali

312) *Why can it very easily be
separated into two parts ?*

    A) It comprises rice and bacon
    B) It consists of pasta and fish
    C) It's a type of stew
    D) It's a savoury pudding

313) A popular type of green
salad leaf is known as what ?

   A) Missile
   B) Torpedo
   C) Bomb
   D) Rocket

314) *The taste of this leaf is said
to be what generally ?*

   A) Very garlicky
   B) Honey sweet
   C) Very salty
   D) Slightly peppery

315) *Pâté* is traditionally made in a deep earthen-
ware dish with a tight-fitting lid called a what ?

   A) Ternary
   B) Terrine
   C) Terylene
   D) Terrarium

316) *Before going into the oven, this dish,
in turn, is normally placed in a pan of
hot water called a what ?*

   A) Barium
   B) Bain-marie
   C) Barramundi
   D) Banshee

317) *Angostura bitters* is a brown-red, spicy type of what ?

    A) Tonic
    B) Onion
    C) Vodka
    D) Potato

318) *It was originally used as a medicinal cure for what ?*

    A) Myopia
    B) Arthritis
    C) Fever
    D) Chilblains

319) *How is it most commonly employed today ?*

    A) To flavour sauces
    B) To enrich curries
    C) To flavour drinks
    D) To bulk out meat dishes

320) *Which country does it hail from originally ?*

    A) Bangladesh
    B) Romania
    C) Malawi
    D) Venezuela

321) *Chicory*, or *endive*, is a white and crispy type of what ?

    A) Salad vegetable
    B) Dried meat
    C) Stale bread snack
    D) Chilli sausage

322) *It is generally accepted to taste how ?*

    A) Slightly bitter
    B) Very spicy
    C) Tasteless
    D) Very sweet

323) Three-star *cognac* is aged for how long traditionally ?

    A) More than 30 years
    B) Between three and five years
    C) Between 10 and 20 years
    D) Up to 10 weeks

324) *What is the usual ageing time for VSOP (Very Superior Old Pale) cognac ?*

    A) Up to 15 weeks
    B) Between six and 10 months
    C) Between five and 15 years
    D) Over 20 years

325) *What is the minimum ageing period for Napoléon cognac ?*

    A) Ten years
    B) Five to six months
    C) Five to six years
    D) Thirty years

326) *Gruyère is a very popular type of cheese well known for its what ?*

    A) Crumbly texture
    B) Mild taste
    C) Blue veins
    D) Pungent smell

327) *Which country does it come from originally ?*

    A) The Netherlands
    B) Finland
    C) Switzerland
    D) Canada

328) *What is it primarily made up of ?*

    A) Sheep's milk
    B) Goat's milk
    C) Buffalo's milk
    D) Cow's milk

329) *Sencha, Hojicha, Gyokuro* and *Matcha* are popular types of Japanese what ?

A) Tea
B) Coffee
C) Milkshake
D) Fish snack

330) A *Chinese* frying pan with a rounded bottom and domed lid is called a what ?

A) Whorl
B) Wok
C) Woad
D) Wold

331) Made with spiced meat or fish, what is a *quenelle* ?

A) A burger
B) A pasty
C) A sausage
D) A dumpling

332) *What is the traditional way to cook one ?*

A) By oven roasting it
B) By poaching it in water
C) By deep frying it
D) By shallow frying it

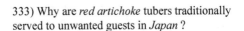

333) Why are *red artichoke* tubers traditionally served to unwanted guests in *Japan* ?

    A) They have a purgative effect
    B) They make guests merry
    C) They make guests ravenous
    D) They have a fatal effect

334) A *béchamel* sauce made to accompany certain dishes is normally what colour ?

    A) Yellow
    B) Orange
    C) White
    D) Brown

335) *What are three fundamental elements to this sauce ?*

    A) Butter, flour and juice
    B) Olive oil, seeds and juice
    C) Butter, flour and milk
    D) Olive oil, seeds and butter

336) *Besides onion, what else are these normally infused with ?*

    A) Ginger, nutmeg, garlic
    B) Peppercorns, nutmeg, bay
    C) Rosemary, thyme, bay
    D) Parsley, sage, tarragon

337) The percentage of *cocoa* in chocolate varies
from about two per cent in white chocolate
to around how much in dark ?

A) Four per cent
B) Seventy per cent
C) Sixteen per cent
D) Forty per cent

338) *Chives* are a grassy, onion-
flavoured type of what ?

A) Nut
B) Spice
C) Fruit
D) Herb

339) *How are chives typically
served in a summer setting ?*

A) Chopped into salads
B) Deep fried with fish
C) Grilled with steaks
D) Boiled with pasta

340) *Oxidised* beer, wine or cider used
as a *'condiment'* is known as what ?

A) Vintner
B) Vinegar
C) Vino
D) Vinaigrette

341) *Cinnamon* is a popular spice
obtained from where exactly ?

    A) The bark of a tree
    B) The leaves of a plant
    C) The stems of a flower
    D) The roots of a plant

342) *Which part of the world is
it normally associated with ?*

    A) Asia
    B) Africa
    C) Europe
    D) South America

343) *Which two forms is it now
usually available in ?*

    A) Leaves and powder
    B) Leaves and sticks
    C) Sticks and powder
    D) Sticks and buds

344) *Risotto* is a dish where meat or fish,
vegetables, butter and stock combine
with what other main ingredient ?

    A) Rice
    B) Chickpeas
    C) Spaghetti
    D) Breadcrumbs

345) *Which country is risotto traditionally associated with ?*

    A) Belgium
    B) Saudi Arabia
    C) Spain
    D) Italy

346) How are difficult-to-locate natural *truffles* tracked down by those who seek them ?

    A) By sight
    B) By scent
    C) By sound
    D) By luck

347) *Which two types of animal are normally used to find them ?*

    A) Geese and ducks
    B) Sheep and goats
    C) Pigs and dogs
    D) Horses and hens

348) *Pistou* is a French version of a popular Italian what ?

    A) Pasta sauce
    B) Dessert
    C) Liqueur
    D) Rice dish

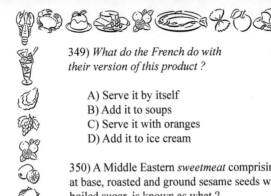

349) *What do the French do with their version of this product ?*

    A) Serve it by itself
    B) Add it to soups
    C) Serve it with oranges
    D) Add it to ice cream

350) A Middle Eastern *sweetmeat* comprising, at base, roasted and ground sesame seeds with boiled sugar, is known as what ?

    A) Halal
    B) Halva
    C) Hakea
    D) Haka

351) *Ricotta* is a cheese whose colour and texture can best be described as what ?

    A) White and crumbly
    B) Orange and waxy
    C) Yellow and crumbly
    D) White and waxy

352) *Which two animals are used to supply milk for ricotta ?*

    A) Cow and sheep
    B) Buffalo and cow
    C) Goat and buffalo
    D) Goat and sheep

353) What is the more colloquial name for *mâche*, a dark green salad leaf often served whole with its root ?

    A) Lamb's lettuce
    B) Fire lettuce
    C) Elephant's lettuce
    D) Snow lettuce

354) What colour is the sauce traditionally served with a *fricassée* stew of meat or fish ?

    A) Yellow
    B) White
    C) Brown
    D) Black

Answers

1) **B** *Holes*
2) **B** *Switzerland*
3) **D** *Firm*
4) **B** *Tainted by a decaying cork*
5) **A** *Ring*
6) **C** *Syrah*
7) **A** *Shiraz*
8) **D** *Calzone*
9) **B** *Norway*
10) **C** *Sparkling*
11) **A** *Cheese*
12) **A** *Courgette*
13) **C** *Doux*
14) **A** *Nebuchadnezzar*
15) **D** *Twenty*
16) **B** *Sixteen*
17) **C** *South Africa*
18) **A** *Germany*
19) **B** *Coffee bean*
20) **D** *Shellfish*
21) **C** *White*
22) **A** *Veal*
23) **D** *Anchovy*
24) **B** *Shells*
25) **C** *Saffron*
26) **D** *Grain*
27) **B** *Whiskey*
28) **A** *Maize*
29) **D** *Italian dessert*
30) **B** *Fungi*
31) **C** *Underground*
32) **D** *Three*
33) **C** *Samosa*

34) **B** *Cocktail*
35) **C** *White rum*
36) **A** *Ribbons*
37) **D** *Beef*
38) **B** *A very young wine*
39) **C** *Greece*
40) **B** *Strong, pungent aroma*
41) **B** *Italy*
42) **C** *New World*
43) **B** *Mediterranean*
44) **A** *Twists*
45) **D** *Christmas*
46) **D** *Chilli*
47) **A** *Stew*
48) **D** *Hungary*
49) **B** *Herdsman's meat*
50) **C** *Growth or crop*
51) **C** *The lowest standard*
52) **B** *The highest standard*
53) **D** *Appetizers*
54) **A** *Before the meal*
55) **B** *Sturgeon*
56) **A** *Blinis*
57) **C** *Soured cream*
58) **D** *Beluga*
59) **A** *Caspian and Black seas*
60) **B** *Lumpfish roe*
61) **C** *The Netherlands*
62) **A** *Red*
63) **B** *Gouda*
64) **A** *Year of production*
65) **A** *It's a blend of vintages*
66) **B** *Soup*

67) **D** *Cream*
68) **D** *Chilled*
69) **A** *Dessert*
70) **B** *Italy*
71) **C** *Alcoholic spirit*
72) **C** *Scandinavia*
73) **A** *Grain*
74) **A** *Long, thin flat strands*
75) **D** *Small tongues*
76) **C** *Pitta*
77) **B** *It can be split and filled*
78) **B** *German Rhine*
79) **A** *Skewered on sticks*
80) **B** *Malaysia and Indonesia*
81) **A** *Peanut sauce*
82) **A** *Liver*
83) **C** *Poached or braised*
84) **B** *The birds are force fed*
85) **B** *White*
86) **B** *France*
87) **A** *Ullage*
88) **D** *Wine*
89) **A** *Germany*
90) **D** *Frozen by frost*
91) **B** *Chowder*
92) **B** *Blue*
93) **A** *England*
94) **A** *Cow's milk*
95) **C** *Sausage*
96) **D** *Cured pork or beef*
97) **D** *Fabada*
98) **B** *Dry white wine*
99) **B** *Soya beans*
100) **B** *Vegetarians*
101) **A** *Japan*
102) **D** *Sage*
103) **B** *White wine*

104) **D** *In seasoned oak casks*
105) **C** *Western France*
106) **A** *A Screwdriver*
107) **B** *Fish*
108) **D** *Japan*
109) **A** *Soy sauce*
110) **A** *Cornmeal*
111) **A** *Boiled or baked*
112) **D** *Sparkling*
113) **A** *Noble rot*
114) **B** *In sheets*
115) **C** *Bread*
116) **C** *Germany*
117) **C** *Snack*
118) **A** *Cured ham*
119) **B** *Eight months to two years*
120) **C** *Parma*
121) **B** *Nan*
122) **A** *Teardrop*
123) **D** *In a tandoori oven*
124) **D** *Wheels*
125) **C** *Crocuses*
126) **C** *Stigmas*
127) **A** *Dumplings*
128) **A** *Tomato sauce*
129) **B** *Dry vermouth*
130) **B** *A green olive*
131) **C** *On a skewer*
132) **B** *Lamb*
133) **A** *A pitta bread*
134) **D** *Chardonnay*
135) **D** *Parcels*
136) **C** *Nutmeg*
137) **A** *Italy*
138) **A** *Distilled wine grape remains*
139) **B** *Mozzarella*
140) **B** *Pizzas*

141) **C** *Ouzo*
142) **B** *It becomes milky*
143) **A** *Julienne*
144) **D** *Harvey Wallbanger*
145) **B** *Butterflies*
146) **C** *Tomato or spinach*
147) **B** *Tapas*
148) **D** *Noisette*
149) **A** *Zinfandel*
150) **B** *Osso bucco*
151) **C** *Large tubes*
152) **D** *Meat filling and sauce*
153) **B** *Armagnac*
154) **B** *Forty years*
155) **C** *Small fish*
156) **A** *It is dried in the sun*
157) **D** *Beetroot*
158) **D** *Eastern Europe*
159) **B** *Feta*
160) **C** *Baklava*
161) **A** *Potatoes*
162) **A** *Thinly sliced with cream*
163) **B** *Daiquiri*
164) **C** *Flat bread*
165) **D** *Garlic and rosemary*
166) **B** *Haricot*
167) **D** *Parmesan*
168) **D** *Freshly grated*
169) **A** *Confit*
170) **C** *More of the same fat*
171) **C** *India*
172) **C** *Pastry*
173) **A** *The West Indies*
174) **B** *Raw salmon*
175) **A** *Mustard and dill*
176) **C** *Sausage*
177) **C** *Beef, pork or veal*

178) **A** *Tequila*
179) **C** *A pinch of salt*
180) **B** *Champagne*
181) **D** *Penne*
182) **A** *Sushi*
183) **A** *Pickled ginger/horseradish*
184) **B** *Spiced hors d' oeuvre*
185) **B** *Small bite*
186) **B** *Ladies' fingers*
187) **C** *Blackcurrants*
188) **A** *Kir Royale*
189) **D** *Roquefort*
190) **D** *In caves*
191) **A** *Small curved tubes*
192) **C** *Cabbage*
193) **C** *Teriyaki*
194) **B** *Rosé*
195) **D** *Blush*
196) **A** *Pine nuts*
197) **C** *Singapore Sling*
198) **A** *Deep fried patties*
199) **B** *Spiced beans or chickpeas*
200) **D** *In pitta bread*
201) **A** *Coriander*
202) **C** *In a pastry case*
203) **B** *Coulis*
204) **C** *Margarita*
205) **B** *Salt around the rim*
206) **B** *Blanquette*
207) **D** *Clarified stock*
208) **D** *Chapatti*
209) **A** *The most popular pasta*
210) **C** *Ginger*
211) **B** *In oiled or buttered paper/foil*
212) **B** *It keeps in juices and flavours*

213) **C** *Mrs Beeton*
214) **A** *1836-1865*
215) **B** *Crudités*
216) **C** *Cheddar*
217) **C** *Cow's milk*
218) **D** *Twelve to 18 months*
219) **B** *Merlot*
220) **A** *Red Bordeaux*
221) **C** *Escoffier*
222) **C** *1847-1935*
223) **A** *Peach Melba*
224) **A** *A female Australian soprano*
225) **A** *Claret*
226) **D** *Soup*
227) **D** *Chilled or iced*
228) **B** *Cumin*
229) **B** *On a skewer*
230) **B** *Dhal*
231) **A** *Corn pancake*
232) **C** *Filled with meat or beans*
233) **C** *Chilli sauce and cheese*
234) **D** *Tapenade*
235) **B** *In pasta sauces*
236) **A** *Rice*
237) **B** *Lightness of taste*
238) **B** *Cream*
239) **C** *Fish fillets and fish stock*
240) **C** *Cuttlefish and its ink*
241) **D** *Goat's milk*
242) **D** *In small rolls*
243) **A** *Its source*
244) **B** *Smorgasbord*
245) **C** *Mushroom*
246) **D** *Squash*
247) **C** *Potato*
248) **C** *Germany*

249) **B** *Vine leaves*
250) **A** *Greece and Turkey*
251) **D** *Wheat*
252) **D** *North Africa*
253) **B** *Chocolate*
254) **A** *Lower fat content/no caffeine*
255) **A** *A very high standard*
256) **A** *Blue ribbon*
257) **B** *The top order of knighthood*
258) **D** *Hollandaise*
259) **C** *Between main courses*
260) **C** *A sorbet or small salad*
261) **A** *Anise*
262) **D** *Pastis and ouzo*
263) **C** *India*
264) **C** *Flour*
265) **C** *France*
266) **A** *Italy*
267) **A** *Sausage*
268) **A** *Black pudding*
269) **D** *Coarse pâté*
270) **D** *As an hors d'oeuvre*
271) **B** *Spirit*
272) **A** *A variety of fruit*
273) **A** *Ice cold*
274) **B** *Red wine*
275) **C** *White bread*
276) **D** *Italy*
277) **C** *Mushrooms*
278) **B** *Florentine*
279) **B** *Spinach was a regional crop*
280) **A** *Smoked cod's roe*
281) **A** *Greece*
282) **B** *Pale pink*

283) **A** *Pinot noir*
284) **D** *Tahini*
285) **C** *Hummous*
286) **C** *Puréed chickpeas*
287) **C** *Gumbo*
288) **C** *Okra*
289) **D** *Fish*
290) **D** *Smoked haddock*
291) **B** *Sheep's stomach*
292) **B** *Scotland*
293) **B** *Burns Night, January 25*
294) **A** *Avocado*
295) **B** *Tortillas*
296) **C** *Meat, fruit and alcohol*
297) **C** *Zen Buddhism*
298) **D** *Melted cheese*
299) **A** *Beef tenderloin*
300) **A** *Two months*
301) **C** *Sliced thinly*
302) **D** *Mushroom*
303) **C** *Nice and south east France*
304) **C** *Anchovies*
305) **A** *Cracked wheat*
306) **A** *Tabbouleh*
307) **B** *Switzerland*
308) **A** *Gherkins*
309) **D** *Cabernet Sauvignon*
310) **C** *Soup and main dish*
311) **A** *France*
312) **C** *It's a type of stew*
313) **D** *Rocket*
314) **D** *Slightly peppery*
315) **B** *Terrine*
316) **B** *Bain-marie*
317) **A** *Tonic*
318) **C** *Fever*
319) **C** *To flavour drinks*

320) **D** *Venezuela*
321) **A** *Salad vegetable*
322) **A** *Slightly bitter*
323) **B** *Between three and five years*
324) **C** *Between five and 15 years*
325) **D** *Thirty years*
326) **B** *Mild taste*
327) **C** *Switzerland*
328) **D** *Cow's milk*
329) **A** *Tea*
330) **B** *Wok*
331) **D** *A dumpling*
332) **B** *By poaching it in water*
333) **A** *They have a purgative effect*
334) **C** *White*
335) **C** *Butter, flour and milk*
336) **B** *Peppercorns, nutmeg, bay*
337) **B** *Seventy per cent*
338) **D** *Herb*
339) **A** *Chopped into salads*
340) **B** *Vinegar*
341) **A** *The bark of a tree*
342) **A** *Asia*
343) **C** *Sticks and powder*
344) **A** *Rice*
345) **D** *Italy*
346) **B** *By scent*
347) **C** *Pigs and dogs*
348) **A** *Pasta sauce*
349) **B** *Add it to soups*
350) **B** *Halva*
351) **A** *White and crumbly*
352) **A** *Cow and sheep*
353) **A** *Lamb's lettuce*
354) **B** *White*

Acknowledgments

Thanks are due to several sources as either first or second references but mostly to the following: The Oxford English Dictionary; Collins English Dictionary; Reader's Digest: Illustrated Dictionary of Essential Knowledge; The Really Quite Good British Cookbook; Food Facts, A Study of Food and Nutrition; Food Facts For The Kitchen Front.